Yoga with Alef

ReMind™

Mara M. Zimmerman

Balboa Press books may be ordered through booksellers or by contacting:

Balboa Press
A Division of Hay House
1663 Liberty Drive
Bloomington, IN 47403
www.balboapress.com
844-682-1282

Interior Image Credit: Mara M. Zimmerman

ISBN: 979-8-7652-4242-1 (sc)
ISBN: 979-8-7652-4243-8 (e)

Library of Congress Control Number: 2023909597

Print information available on the last page.

Balboa Press rev. date: 06/09/2023

Yoga with Alef

A guided meditation honoring
the wisdom of both traditions,
and their individual and universal
potential to inspire people
of all walks of life.

Enjoy

Good posture. Balanced Breathing.

Breathe in…breathe out…inhale…exhale.

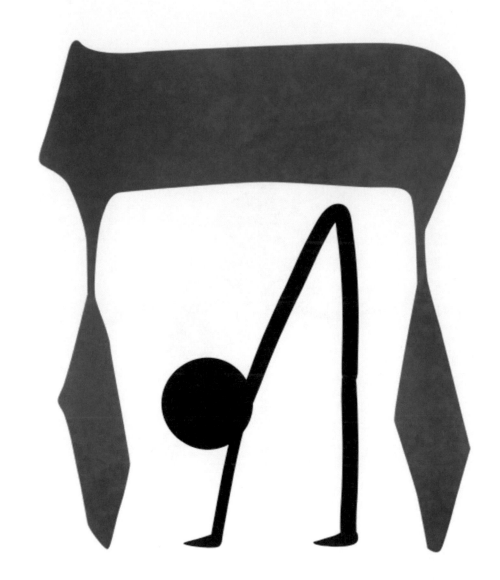

14

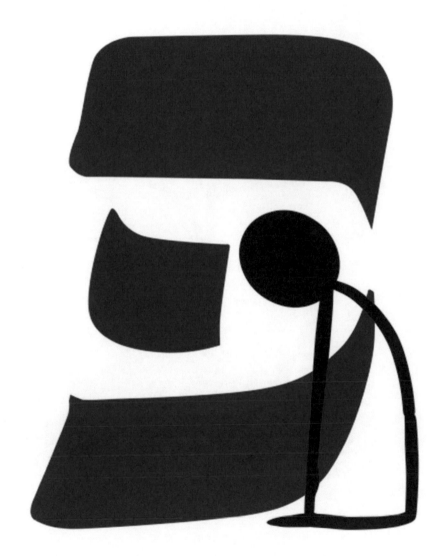

Sun-Surya-Shemesh

Yoga-Union

Alef-Oneness

Ot-letter-sign

Namaste-A peaceful greeting

Om-A peaceful sound

Shalom-A peaceful greeting and a peaceful sound

Ardha Chandrasana-Variation-Half-Moon Pose

Adho Mukha Vrksasana-Handstand Pose-Advanced

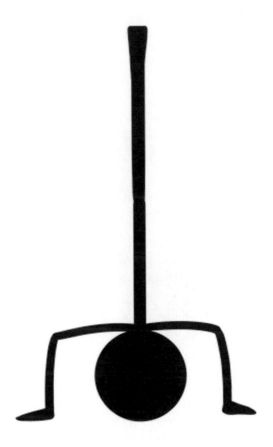

Salamba Sirsasana-Supported Headstand Pose-Advanced

Baddha Konasana Sirsasana-Butterfly Headstand Pose-Advanced

Balasana-Child's Pose-Calm-Cool

Baddha Konasana-Seated Butterfly Pose

Modified Sarvangasana-Modified Shoulder Stand Pose-Pause

Savasana-Resting Pose-Advanced

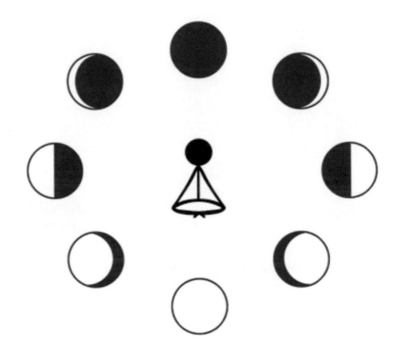

New Beginnings

Chai-Life-Chai-Tea

Namaste. Shalom.

ReMind

Author's Note

Each Hebrew letter and Yoga pose have individual and collective value. Hebrew words are read from right to left. Movements pictured on one side of the body are intended to be repeated on both sides for balance. Movements can be done with the body, or in stillness, as a mindful visual.

Glossary

Transliterated Hebrew letters and sounds
Transliterated Sanskrit and English names of Yoga poses

Alef-Silent-Trikonasana-Triangle pose

Bet-B-V-Modified Dandasana-Modified seated staff pose or seated good posture

Gimmel-G-Modified Virabhadrasana 1-Modified warrior 1 pose

Dalet-D-Modified Virabhadrasana 3-Modified warrior 3 pose

Hey-H-Modified Padahastasana-Modified hand to toe or leg pose

Vav-V-Tadasana-Mountain pose or standing good posture

Zayin-Z-Vinyasa-Flow of movements with breath from side to side and pose to pose

Chet-Ch-Uttanasana-Standing folding forward bend

Tet-T-Navasana-Boat pose

Yud-Y-Balasana-Child's pose

Kaf-K-Kh-Janu Sirsasana- Seated tree pose or modified head to knee pose

Lamed-L-Utkatasana-Chair pose

Mem-M-Setu Bandhasana- Bridge pose

Nun-N-Dandasana-Seated staff pose or seated good posture

Samech-S-Dhanurasana-Bow pose

Ayin-Silent-Vasisthasana-Side plank pose

Pey-P-F-Ustrasana-Camel pose

Tzadeh-Ts-Modified Supta Padangusthasana-Modified reclining extended hand to toe or leg pose

Kuf-K-Q-Vrksasana-Tree pose

Resh--R-Ardha Chandrasana-Half moon pose

Shin-Sh-S-Modified Dhanurasana-Modified bow pose

Tav-T-Marjaryasana-Bitilasana-Cat-Cow-pose or Bharmanasana-Table top pose

Final Kaf—Kh-Modified Adho Mukha Svanasana-Modified downward facing dog pose

Final Mem-M-Adho Mukha Svanasana-Downward facing dog pose

Final Nun-N-Samasthiti-Standing pause, stillness

Final Fey-F-Natarajasana-Dancer pose

Final Tzadeh-Ts-Utthita Tadasana-Star pose

About the Author

Mara M. Zimmerman has been teaching Yoga, Meditation and Mindfulness to all ages in educational and therapeutic spaces throughout her career. She is the creator of ReMind, a program for optimal well-being for all ages.

More books by the Author

ReMind: Building Rocks of Mindfulness with Stepping Stones

ReMind: Building Rocks of Mindfulness with Jewish Stepping Stones

ReMind: Rooms with Chairs

and

How to Meditate and Why

For more information, please visit
maramzimmerman.com

Printed in the United States
by Baker & Taylor Publisher Services